Move Over
Shakespeare

TALES FROM THE BARON

BILLY J. BARNUM

PAGE PUBLISHING, INC.
New York, NY

First originally published by Page Publishing, Inc. 2019

ISBN 978-1-64544-602-6 (Paperback)
ISBN 978-1-64544-603-3 (Digital)

Printed in the United States of America

The Unforgotten Tale (Black Rose)

The rose that burns before my eyes
Will soon my friend again arise
My soul it burns with strong desire
To find who lit the rose on fire

My life has been a tragic waste
I do not bleed, but blood I taste
The rose was black, like night my child
Like the stallion I rode, when I was wild

The sun's no more, the earth I see
Will linger in my memory
When I am gone, please carry on
And journey till the quest is done

This magic seed that seems be stilled
Was once the rose that evil killed
My fondest wish I now behold
The rose it grows so true and bold

And black as night, just like it was
And give it light, and give it love
If tales were told about the thorn
I'll tell you one, but do be warned

The rose it burned, so big and high
That reached into the mystic sky
The world it shook, the sky went black
The children cried, and the moon it cracked

I feared this once, but I never knew
That a sky so black, was once so blue
The fate you see is in your hand
So go my son, and make a plan

The rose it grows one day again
But only you will know just when
And when it does, all that you see
Will only be a memory

All Is Black

A puzzled mind, I come to you
And tell you that it's wrong
I felt it coming all along
I felt it all along

The crush I lay upon your shoulders
The wind she's blown away
To the north or parallel
Nightfall comes and snuffs the day

Now that all has turned to black
Simply just another hue
What a strangely, oddly vision
See the sky has eyes of blue

Staring out into the night
Empty sky with empty faces
Can't imagine what you see
Emptiness with empty traces

Fade away into the void
Nullify this awful pain
Wash away these reasons being
Wash away with heaven's rain

The Dream of the Lion

I once in my life had the dream of the lion
When I woke up last night all I seen, you were cryin'
The blood of a soldier
The dreams of a fool
And the mightiest gods making up their own rules
The knights of the justice have beckoned and gone
The desire of angels from morning to dawn
And the sigh of a prisoner where people are dying
All are a part of the dream of the lion

With spirits bewildered with nowhere to go
And the scream of a pirate as he loses his soul
Where lightning is striking and people are scared
There's a war in the graveyard just like no one cared
If the love of an angel can't stop all this crying
Then this is a part of the dream of the lion

The shed of a tear and the freedom behold
With famish and hunger of both young and old
For the valiant get stronger and the sick getting weak
And the slyness of war dogs killing off the whole fleet
And the preachers are praying for the mightiest hope
That tomorrow will come without all this mope
The miracle of saints couldn't save them from dying
They said it was all just the dream of the lion

Crazy Skies

The starlit sky which I inscribe
Remind me of the Blackfeet Tribe
The white man tried to take his land
From now till death he take his stand

"I shall not leave, and I shall not go
This land is my pride, where my children shall grow"
And grow they will till the mightiest of man
And then I think you'll understand

Why we have fought through many moons
And many crazy skies
With hopes that someday there'll be a world
Where no one has to die

But not enough for me to ask
I never seen it true
The white man came, like winds so swift
And left here black and blue

The Pond with No Reflection

Have you ever heard the tale
Of the pond with no reflection
It came to me on a stormy night
Of a past life recollection

Only those men brave and true
Would stop to circle near
The pond that wise men stayed away from
Done out of spite and fear

Near the pond a mighty tree
So big it wouldn't die
And in the bark initials carved
From fools who've lastly cried

One day a knight bravely challenged
A myth from years ago
He took his horse and sat upon it
And rode down devil's row

The pond grew nearer, his heart beat faster
The jesters head all filled with laughter

"I have a new joke I will tell"
When you should fall from grace
Your armor lay there like a shell
Your helmet bear no face

Then I will pass this tale on
To every man I see
And when they ask, "Have you seen John?"
I'll reply, the last I've seen of him
He was standing near the mighty tree
Carving his initials
If only he just let it be
But, he chose the wrong direction
And hastily joined the ranks of fools
For the pond with no reflection!

Am I, I Am

See me now for what I am, am I, I'm just a man
Who lives and breathes like everyone else
Two feet how shall I stand
If I shall fail, step out of line
I'll do the best I can
But some people think, that I am not
    Am I? Yes, I Am

For structure is the principle
For everything I stand
And light that guides me, hides the key
So once again I ask myself
    Am I? Oh yes, I Am!

It lies there deep inside my mind
So close but out of reach
And if the master tells me to use it
I promise my soul, I'll teach
I feel inside I've lived before
In some forgotten land
And if I did, would the question still arise
    Am I? Yes I Am!

And now I stand before my peers
And now I make my stand
I motion the motive
That motions the jury
That motions against what I stand
And the verdict that still lies in front of me
    Am I? You bet I Am!

The Unknown Poet

When life is through, and I look back
I'll have to sit and wonder
Of all the fools, who've passed me by
How many have heard the thunder

I cried out loud! And built my blocks
So I could step up higher
And look down upon the doubtful ones
Who'll someday call me sire

I speak the truth of what I know
But no one seems to hear
So I keep my talent hid inside
Until I can send my message clear

I reckon I'll be left behind
Behind, like all the rest
But, as it is told in early times
His last laugh is his best

Maybe I'll just fade away
And wither like the wind, that drifts to the sea
Or maybe years and years from now
Someone will finally set me free

They'll stumble upon a dusty book
Ancient from years ago
And feed their curiosity
"What's inside, I have to know!"

I'll read a verse! Just one page
At an instance I'm hooked
I find myself upon the stage

My instincts in a state of awe!
My fists were clenched with rage
The eerie feelings within the binder
I dread to turn the final page

I turned the page, and found a note
I opened it, inside it read:

"To whom, to all it may concern
My book has gone unnoticed
To whom, to you it may concern
Are the chosen one with destiny

Thank you for the service
Thank you for the favor
And if you know just what I mean
In time, I'll thank you later!"

The Color Gray

Take me to a special place
A place so far away
A place to where my soul escapes
A place where I can stay

I'll run through flowers
Climb up trees
Anything my desires, please

Not of this world
For it's left me stray
Not of this world
No time of day

Careless in my ventures
Never looking back
No one looks at no one wrong
No such word, too late! Attack!

Never thought a whole new place
Would erupt a sculptured demon
Giving all this universe
A different kind of meaning

Don't go near the light
Don't wake up today
Don't know why the echo falls
Don't know what, the color gray!

Is Anyone There?

I feel I'm lost within a dream
But waking seems too hard for me
I tried, I tried with all my heart
I tried with all my soul
But the game master holds the key of life
And back to start I go
I never thought I'd be afraid
Of the dream within reality
I feel the earth, it shakes with fear
My god, my god, is anyone there?
As I lay my head upon the ground
I bleed to death, I die
But the world's still spinnin' round and round
And no one knows I even died
And no one knows the reasons why
The world's still spinnin' round and round
My god I wish I've cried

Where's the Man?

The light that guides me
Through the bloodshed field
I pray to you please do not yield

'Cause I have not sinned, and I cannot find
The madness within this wretched mind

Does it reflect of days gone by?
Or can I ask the reasons why?

Why do they fight? Why do they bleed?
Has hell broke loose for its own need?

The answer's clear but where's the man
Who has the answer where does he stand?

Someday you know he will be found
But by then I will not be around.

Do What Me You Will!

Sacrifice me now
I cannot wait a minute longer
For if you leave me standing here
My bloodline grows much ever stronger

Bring me down now, to the pit
Bring me down for good
For if you leave me kneeling
I'll once remember, how I stood

Lead me on, to the hangin' post
Tie the blindfold tight
For if you leave me restless
I may remember, I once had sight

Stab me with your dagger
Turn it once or twice
For if I come back and haunt you, sir
Will that I ask you, will that suffice?

Reflections

Reflect me now, and I will see
The man that lies inside of me
Is he gentle? Is he kind?
Or does he have an evil mind?

Can you really see the man
That hides behind the mask?
I know this time the table's turned
Why do you think I'd ask?

Reflections in the waves
Is a picture-perfect you
With one swift motion of the hand
It all is done and through

The Missing Piece

Can you teach me how to fly?
I'm not sure, but I can try
Then can you teach me how to soar?
I don't know, son, I'll try once more
Can you teach me how to see?
Reach deeper and deeper, and maybe you'll see
Then can you teach me how to hear?
I'll try my son, just lend me your ear
Can you teach me how to walk?
Rise to your feet, and move as you talk
And can you teach me how to think
That, my son, I cannot do
For every puzzle that seems undone
The missing piece, lies within you, my son

Painted Face

I'll put on a painted face
My friends could never tell
And every time I see them
I'll say I'm doing well

But soon the makeup will start to run
And ruin my disguise
They'll see the frown that lies within
And see my fragile eyes

You see, I have to wear this face
It's the only one I know
Where I can fool the world
For a while, please don't tell

So I will wear this painted face
The world will never see
What I am hiding, beneath my skin
And deep inside of me

Never

Long ago, and far away
There lived a simple man
Who gave away a thousand dreams
And did the best he can

Then one day, he started to
Take them back, one by one
All of the sudden, people realized
That life was just not fun

I wonder why, that kind old man
Has taken back our precious dreams
Silence now has taken over
Leaves have left the trees

If we could all, get together
And show him that there's more out there
Then maybe, just maybe
He'll show us that he really cares

You see, some people bottle up
The things that hurt them most
Let's throw a party, in his honor
And we will be his host

We'll show him that we all are here
In spirit, and in life
And make him feel good inside
And feel good to be alive

And then the kind old man
Will have a dream to call his own
And the dreams before that we once knew
Back to us, again will have flown

And then the things he's kept inside
No longer will he have to hide
Never fear to open up
Never

The Sign of the Times

This my friend is the sign of the times
And you will see what's about to come
So hold on tight and close your eyes
And don't forget to spit out your gum

Changes coming way too fast
Much too fast to handle
Hurry! Rush! Get out the way
From the dropping of the anvil

You're standing still and all is calm
Abruptly everything starts to get warm
You can't believe what your eyes can see
You're right inside the eye of the storm

So hold on tight and close your eyes
And don't forget to spit out your gum
'Cause this my friend is the sign of the times
And now you know what's about to come

Serenity

Serenity, it's something that I really need
But something that I rarely find
I know it's somewhere, it has to be
It's somewhere deep inside my mind

One time I reached serenity
But just before I did
Collisions formed in front of me
And then I ran and hid

Meteors were bursting
And the sky's without a sun
And the banging of the thunder crashed
All that remained, had come undone

Swirling winds, and reckless rage
Of competence and devastation
Wish that I could turn the page
And help this nightmare wicked nation

Soon I was oblivious
To all that was around me
Father, may I come aboard?
Now that you have found me

This is where I drifted off
And had this peaceful, easy dream
Where all was one and one was all
And so was I, serenity

Don't Wait for Anyone

The magician can't do his magic anymore
I wonder why
The circus is always full of laughter
But I witnessed a tragedy, I seen the clowns cry

Why are they so sad? I do not know
But I look for the answer, where the wild winds blow

Noah floats upon his ark
That's lost upon the sea
And all the animals are in pairs
Except for one I see

Did the other get lost?
Did the other survive?
Did the other one vanish?
Or is he barely alive?

He said, "You'll never find out, my son
Because chance can't rule your fate
But loneliness, consumes your body
And by then it's just too late

Live your life, find your dream
But don't wait for anyone
'Cause they'll just hold you down
And then it'll be too late for you too

Why would I tell you this?
Why? Do you know why?
If I was not the man I am
I might break down and cry

The only thing that rules your fate
Is you, and only you
So hold your head up high, my son
And stop your feeling blue

The magicians, the clowns
Everyone will perform again someday
Just a little time, for their hearts to mend
And all their fears will fly away."

Someday I'll be King

I am flying high
And nothing's gonna hold me back
I thought that I had seen the queen
But it was just the jack

And he was acting like the king
But boy was he surprised
The king was just a mask he wore
It was the joker in disguise

He said, "I could make you famous"
I know you heard it all before
But this time I won't joke around
So count the points, and add the score

I may be just a jack
But someday, I will be king
And maybe I'll select you to make me laugh
Now wouldn't that be something

Ground control I'm coming down
Please don't ever let me crash
The deck is stacked against me, man
The answer's written on the back

Demon in My Dreams

I want to sleep, but I just can't
I never know just where it takes me
'Cause in my dreams, I've seen some things
The demon always tries to rape me

Not in a physical sense
But to take something without consent
It's hard enough for me to describe
And what he tries to take, I must repent

You'll never take me, not alive
I'll never let you take me, no!
I'll fight until my body's lifeless
And even then, you won't take my soul

I'll rise above, and I will conquer
'Cause I don't want to ever go
A tug-of-war, just hold on tight
The seed I plant, will start to grow

Carry on, my child
And always remember I was here
Make the tree grow big and strong
And never ever have no fear

One by One

Now's the time to do the things
You want to do in life
'Cause when you're gone, it's just too late
And everything just passes by

Don't let nothing pass you by
Then you will regret it
And if you want something bad enough
Just go out and get it

This is for you, the reader
I'm writing this for you
In hopes this poem wakes you up
And makes you do what you must do

By the time you read this poem
I may be long gone
But I will have my words in ink
And they will carry on

I want you to do the same
Now go, make a plan and get it done
And pass these words of wisdom on
We'll build their courage, one by one

No Matter What, I'll Be Here

Reckless, in a world that seems so simple
All within the realms of reality
Leaving well enough alone
No such thing, not for me

I walked beyond the barrier
But I could not break through
I heard the sound of thunder
And seen the lightning too

Traveling at the speed of sound
I see the Milky Way
I've never seen the world so dark
I can't remember, light of day

I entered into a tunnel
Far beyond the earth
And pictures flashed before me
They were pictures of my birth

And then I escaped from daydreams
That stumbled into nightmares
And pictures of my death appeared
Do you think that I was scared?

I felt the dehydration
While walking through the desert
Sand was red, and scorching hot
My skin was raw, and it was burnt

But through it all I have maintained
To always keep my will
And no matter what happens, come hell or high water
I will be here still!

Siamese Dreams

Every time I lay to sleep
I seem to have these Siamese dreams

One is blissful, angels singing
One can't describe, the pain it's bringing

Now I'm walking, feel so good, the best I've ever felt
A strange presence, he does me harm, the sky begins to melt

Now I'm strolling, at the park, peacefulness encumbers me
A fallen star, burns to the earth, light so bright I cannot see

I'm on a train, rolling smoothly, all is well and calm
The track divides, the train collides, I think of Vietnam

The dreams I have drive me crazy
Not knowing where they come from
But all the world has Siamese dreams
And in the end, all the world will be at one

Blinding Fury

I bask beneath the paper moon
I bask beneath the twinkling sky
A streak of light appears before me
I make my wish, and close my eyes

Oh, father, can you hear me?
To make this wish come true
Down on my knees, and full of sorrow
Please help this world to not be cruel

I've seen the sinners, tears they flow
But in the heart, there's no remorse
I know that you can help them lord
But in their hearts, they must change first

I see the path they choose to go
But my road leads to you
I follow lights that shine so bright
As I look down at the people breaking every rule

I'm sure that they will change their ways
When they see nature's beauty
Inform thy brother, that there is hope
And never say that you're off duty

It now is time for them to start
Before hell encumbers all their hearts
And fury blinding shows its wrath
And rips their souls and lives in half

Run Away

Run away, don't ever come back
Escape is always never
But you just seemed to get so far
Escape is not for clever

Face-to-face, I stand before
Searching for an answer
Drift away upon the stage
Like some forgotten dancer

The mirror cracks, I cannot see
The lines they blur my vision
It often turns to fantasy
Can't face the life I'm living

And after I leave, and see my ways
Were far beyond a doubt
I enter back, at least I try
Run away, run around, run so far, I can't get out

I need a brand-new mirror
So my new eyes could see so clear
'Cause I don't want to run away
I want to face my fears

There's a Hole in the Sky

Trauma emerged from ashes of the innocent
But nobody knew what was wrong
The only sound throughout that was heard
Was the sound of a coveted last lonely song

The bugles played, a tune so bleak
The soldiers march, a bit out of line
The flags they flew, all at half-staff
A smiling face, you could not find

I've never seen such desolation
Well maybe once, but that was in a dream
And all the visions that came to me
I rubbed my eyes to set them free

A man he stood and stared at me
The look of sadness, on his face
I could almost feel what he was thinking
Then back in line, he took his place

I searched the souls, at what dismay
Has brought them to this common ground
Then one by one, just as they stood
They started falling down

The man he looked, his voice with rage, he held his head up high
Pointing towards the universe, then I heard him sigh
Cleared his throat and said to me, "Can't you see, there's a hole in
the sky!"

Splashing in the Puddle

Splashing in the puddle
Mama said to "don't get dirty"
What now are we gonna do
Tell me little birdy

New white shoes
Wore our knickers
Shoes shined up
By old shoe spitters

On the way to go to church
I didn't see it there
I was walking proud, my head held high
I didn't have a care

Then off the curb I stepped
My face it turned befuddled
To my surprise, I stepped into
A big ole dark, black puddle

Oh! What a shame, I turned to say
And Billy fell in too
And then we played a little while
And now our shoes don't look so new

Splashing in the puddle
Mama said to "don't get dirty"
What now are we gonna do?
Tell me little birdy

Alone in the Dark

Alone in the dark
Once again, I cannot sleep
My full restraint, to hold inside
The flood of tears, that I will weep

The lion rages, let me out
The mighty roar is heard
As it echoes through the valley
I take to flight, just like a bird

The hunter seeks, but cannot find
His prey, his one obsession
As dragon fire ignites the forest
The hunter learns his lesson

There are many here among us
Growing rapidly into form
Alone in the dark
When unity could be reborn

Look upon the mountain
Up to its highest peak
Where air is thin, and blood runs cold
That's where you'll find me, that's where I'll be

Sorting out the injustices
That once hold me in chains
Instead of using energy
I quickly think to use my brain

Scaling down the mountain
Misfooted, I lose my grip
Tumbling rapidly toward the ground
They seal me in my crypt

I see them lower me in the ground
I see it very clear
But, god how could this be?
When my body lie so limp, and my soul it is up here

You see, my son, now life's a dream
And when you leave, you then awake
And all your sins, you leave behind
And all the good things, that's what you take!

My Inner Child

Undetect my inner child
No one knows he's there
Sometimes he feels so sad
Whenever he is scared

If the flame, it burns too bright
He feels warm inside
But when he sees the darkest nights
He wants to run and hide

When it snows and cold winds blow
Images of desire consume him
'Cause he really never knows
If anyone will be there for him

A suit of armor, with a golden shield
Exterior looks so tough
Cannot show just what he feels
Not one ounce, that's just too much

So I will leave my inner child
Right where he belongs
Away from everything that's wild
Away from all the wrong

Sycamore Tree

Sycamore tree
Oh! Sycamore tree
How high shall you grow
And how much do you know
I'll bet you've seen things in your life
I couldn't even dream of

Did you see the great depression
And all the wars that rage?
And did you see destruction
And rebirth of another day?

Did you see the sky so blue
And ever so rapidly changing hue?

Did you ever see Santa Claus
Man or myth, come on tell me did you ever
See him or the Mrs. make the suit of bright red cloth

You've been through storms and rain a flutter
You're so old, how old is your mother?

Can you tell me what's in store
For the future that lies ahead?
Or will the saw blade spin toward you
And leave our lives in dread?

Well I must go now, can't you see
How stupid must it look
Me talkin' to a tree
A year will pass and I'll be back
To find out if you'll answer me
For knowledge is the thirst for life
Someday you'll speak, oh! Sycamore tree

Rampage

Bolting thunder, lightning
Crashing to the earth
Running many hundreds of miles
Next stop, planet universe

Destruction in the pathway
Ripping up the ground
Tornado of devastation
Powerful winds, spin 'round and 'round

Eruptions of volcanoes
Melting lava down
High-pitched shrieks, of people's screams
Shattering the speed of sound

Waves are crashing, on the shore
Hovering then falling
The world just seems to've gone awry
Communication's lost, but god was calling

It's too late to be stopped now
At last, the final stage
The world has lost its chance for peace
It now is time for rampage!

(Let It Go) Lost Soul

Do you know just how it feels
To always be unwanted?
The lonely soul trapped in a house
But they all say it's haunted

Wanting to be where you belong
But things are left undone
Struggles within the heart they bear
Loves were lost, nothing won

And they cry out, "Hear me scream"
Eerie but still undaunted
I was left behind, my estranged friend
This house should not be haunted

My presence felt, but never seen
That's how I felt in life
Scars they ran so deep inside
It cut me like a knife

I must move on, I must make peace
It now is time to leave this place

Take me into the shining light
I'm ready take me now
I've been down here for much too long
It's time to take a bow

Receive me in thy kingdom
I now have made amends
I hope that in my next lifetime
This never happens again

Jaded Innocence

A photograph, a skip in time
My mind has once forgot
A queen upon her throne so high
A vision that is not

A virgin, blessed your soul, my dear
A rose that's been untouched
A sacred vow, not to be broken
It seems like much too much

Innocence just seems so jaded
A mask that hides her face
Appears to be invisible
Something is out of place

A truth that once seemed so sincere
A trust was once undoubted
A sun within, a clear blue sky
Has now been overcrowded

Fly a kite, high as you can
And see if the gods can see the tail
To find the truth within you see
You have to learn to read in braille

But, I'm not blind, and still can't see
Your jaded innocence is a far cry from honesty

The Eagle

The sunshine yields in an exhilarating ray
Much more than the sunshine did before thine exhilarating day
Boasting of conquests and duels you have victored
And just before the duel starts, the gent kindly says, "First you, sir"
Just a step before the edge, then all your dreams fall over
You could've hung there for a little while
But when time entraps itself in a bottle
The sands run out, and your hands pry free
And so it goes the eagle is so much like me

Purple Moon

I swear one night, I looked outside
And saw a purple moon
I remember it was late in May
Or maybe it was June

You don't have to believe me, if you don't want to
But I know that's what I saw
I'd just awakened from a dream
And there it was, that's all

You're looking at me strange
But this moon was big and bright
Its glow was kind of wonderful
As it spread across the night

I felt a surge of sudden power
The velvet skies, with moonbeams beaming
I had to stop and check myself
To see if I had still been dreaming

Not a chance, I am awake
I knew that it was true
That I had looked outside that night
And saw a purple moon

Fly Again

Icarus he flies too high to the sun
His wings did burn
And ashes fell upon the earth
For fools who long to yearn

It escapes my mind this tragic horror
What an evil crowd, as they yelled "more"
Eagles often emulate, a lesser known obsession
And gods they cry in fear of life
To ease one's own aggression

Fly me on now, you can try
Rebuild your courage, rebuild and fly
Go and see another day
Go, my child, I will not lead you astray

Something's missing from deep within
So how? Oh how? Do I begin?
You reach down, you reach so low
And extract something from your very soul
And then you carry on, my child
And then you carry on

Once in a While

Once in a while, when things go wrong
I feed upon my pain
Once in a while, when I'm not strong
I almost go insane

Once in a while, when courage is little
I struggle to survive
Once in a while, my bones get so brittle
I barely feel alive

Once in a while, time seems so short
As if that there is none
Once in a while, I feel so threatened
But no one stands before me, threatened by no one

Once in a while, I drift away
Careless of all my thoughts
Once in a while, I sense the dread
Of the wars our fathers have fought

And once in a while, I'd like to have peace
Yeah, once in a while
And once in a while, I don't need nothing
Not even, once in a while

Castaway

Thrown upon the shore
Left for something dead
Anxieties run wild now
Thoughts consume my head

Castaway, I am called now
For they have all forgotten
An aura of self, and righteousness
The spoils of man have rotten

An inner peace of sanctity
No god to rule this land
The king am I, the highest power
One card bequeathed, now deal the hand

Lesser known of all the species
Footprints in the sand
Unmarked letter on wall inscribed
Scatterbrain, strike up the band

List of deeds, of wish-a-ways
And inconsequentials of castaways

Why I Left

Get the machine, and fill it up
And let me climb aboard
Point it toward the nearest star
And make a list of what I'm leaving for

To escape the hate that people feel
To get away from all that's real
To never once again see war
Won't send our children out for more
To see the world from just afar
And never wonder where you are
For from this distance all is calm
Can't hear the sound of dropping bombs
Can't hear the sound of people's screams
From way up here, it's just a dream
Don't ever want to see that stuff
Don't they know enough's enough
A sonic boom the world explodes
World War III, the mother load
I'm glad that I am way up here
'Cause, people down there just didn't care
If they changed their hearts, they could've kept
So this is a short list, of why I left

Hell

The damage to my soul has been struck by lightning fires
Trapped within a void, as the flames grow ever higher
Now you feed the flame as the night ignites desire
Shot to hell with no despair I'm trapped within the fire
Extinguish now cannot take place exhumed, too weak to fight
All my visions disappear, I will be in hell tonight
My head hung low, to the point of lifeless
Spin me round and round, my dear
'cause part of me's not burned yet
through the smoke I see a sign
a hand it reaches toward me
then pushes me beneath the surface
and as I slip away
emptiness consumes my body!
Ashes left and nothing more
Remains swept away
With nothing left to remind
It was a very hard place, it hurts
A very hard place to find!

Why Must It Be?

If life was meant to be again
I'd want to know just why
'Cause the sorrow I've seen, in the blackest of dreams
Haunts me forever, with skies are so black, the sun may be never!

Unheavenly winds, a breeze do I feel
For what has brought forth all this pain?
For the rainbow has faded and god has stopped crying
'Cause the sinners who've sinned are no more, they are dying

With peace on the uprise, uncertain is the world
For an answer will come, through the winds that will swirl
Bringing us hope for the world ever after
And maybe someday, once again you'll hear laughter

The infants, they'll walk
The children, they'll play
The stars shine all night
And the sun out all day

Could this world be real
Or must it come to ends
I entered life a lonely boy
And left a broken man

Grieving for the sins they did
Tortured by the pain
Knowing now we're at the end
Just who will stop this rain?

As years go by, and I reflect
A place that one's called earth
I'll stare into the emptiness
And await the resurrection

Of the new world will be coming
For this the final try
If life was meant to be again
I'd want to know just why!

We Awaken

The lonely hunter walks alone
And searches for his prey
Day turns into nighttime now
Then night turns into day

He hears a ruffling in the brush
He looks and there it stands
A grizzly bear that's ten feet tall
Overshadowing the man

He holds the barrel of the gun
He holds it real tight
Then points it straight between the eyes
And tries with all his might

To pull the trigger, his mind say go
But he cannot comply
Compassion settles over him
The rain it falls and tears he cries

I will wait and watch you live
I can't believe I almost did
The unspeakable, to take a life
I really hope you can forgive

For tomorrow will be a new day
And nothing for granted will be taken
There comes a time in everyone's life
Where something happens, then we awaken

Black or White

Reality, the fist of time
Contracts and then expands
According to the actions of
The speaker's one command

When it's closed, a war is raging
Misfortunes from the palm
Opened up, a state of still
Where everything is calm

It's the hand that rocks the nation
And power is its thirst
And warriors have scarlet daydreams
Fending off its curse

It's the knowledge of a novel
Written there within the lines
And the pages scatter in the wind
With nothing there to bind

For when the book is open
Kindness is an open hand
And when the book is closed
Like the fist, nothing's learned, again

What Is Worst

Sometimes things overcome me
That I cannot control
The things in life I love so much
Once again, I'll lose, I know

Lost in desperation
And the pity is too much
Blood is flowing from my body
Puddling, is just too much

I guess I dug my own hole
But I'm too weak to climb in
Just a shove, I ask of you
And no one's wondering where I've been

Oh! Lonely is the child
That faces the cold alone
I've wandered off, and now I'm dizzy
And I can't find my way back home

Maybe now there is no home
And I've settled in my nest
I've felt the harshness of this world
And to hell with all the rest

Rageless anger, faceless stranger
Hollowed by thy merciless curse
Don't go hang her, I'm in danger
Tell me now please, what is worst

Killer's Instinct

The sights unseen have set upon
The maker of the chosen one
The lights unlit have shone upon
Potential of my father's son

The sacred promise pity's none
The smoking barrel of a gun
The swiftness of a cougar's run
The bitterness has stood in stun

The stance you took, and all you've shun
And everything's connived and cunned
The stake is passed and then you lunge
The line is broken, begin the fun

Write these words, think these thoughts
Do as I shall say
Snags in pieces breaking down
Sanity's a world away

Resistance 'cause I will not fight
I lie there screaming in the night
I guess we'll never know who's right
The journey's traveled, and I have plight

Fateful Journey

The mountains by the ocean shore
Was really something great to see
I ended there one stormy night
And I was trapped unwillingly

I was on a glorious journey
Sun was shining, clouds were few
Sailing to my paradise
Everything was all brand-new

Then suddenly, the clouds were grey
And gods were crying in despair
I lowered my bow, and held on tight
My head was ringing out with fear

Boats were thrown about like toys
Crashing waves were loud as thunder
Wood was being ripped apart
Oh my god! I'm going under

Next thing now that I remember
I awoke upon a shore
On the sand, I lay facedown
Am I alive? I must know more

Then I see this mountain
It was big as big can be
Palm trees swaying, no one's home
I'm all alone, yes it's just me

Maybe things are better now
Much better, since I'm all alone
Soon I'll never understand
Why it wasn't like this, when I was home

Years went by, my soul flies free
There's so much joy, tranquility
And just when I have found myself
Someone comes to rescue me

"I said sorry, I don't want to go"
You can keep your evil world
I found what life is all about
I live my life my flags unfurled

When you go back tell everyone
The end is coming soon
Look to the sky, you'll see the sign
It's when the heavens, swallow the moon

And I'll be here, all by myself
Thinking how you'll never see
The things in life, that are so precious
The things in life, that set you free

The Lurker

Sell your soul? A dollar mate?
I know it's wrong, but I just might
The lurker's never far behind
And all the same, he's out of sight

He tames the people with his fear
Afraid of getting caught
Just a peak, before I go
I really think I ought

Let me in, the little things
That no one else should know
"I'm acting like a peeper now
How did you like the show?"

I know your name, I know your number
I got it all etched inside
With all this knowledge, you might wonder
Why I have to hide

I'm sick and shy and really weird
You wouldn't understand
I've played my part so very well
I'll take a bow, give me a hand

Let the lurker worry none
Autumn time has just begun
Let the lurker fade away
Ghosts within the mist today

Wasted Knowledge

Books unread have sat on shelves
Dusty memories of the past
A wasted knowledge locked inside
Could've held the key to life

One page of thoughts and destined words
Could change your way of thinking
The future's fate may lie within
Catch it quick, the book is sinking

It was there, well in your grasp
But your fingertips were full of fire
The meltdown now has just begun
The angels all have grown real tired

Puppets on a string
Puppeteers control their moves
Trains have hit some coins on tracks
Tense derailment off the grooves

Pieces of a broken dream
Have now all been collected
Except for one, I can't make out
An empty space, I must accept it

Knowledge is here for you to use
So please don't ever waste it
The fruits of life can be such bliss
If you don't try, you'll never taste it

Someone Up Above

Sorrow once, from all that's wrong
Another memory's etched in stone
The feeling that I don't belong
The roads they never lead to home

Winding highways, lost in space
Lost within the universe
Let us pray, amazing grace
Stuck 'cause I forgot the verse

Praise, to all I've never seen
And all that I believe
Take me, places never been
Untrue thoughts conceived

Restless nights, shooting stars
Spell my destiny
Written clear, and very large
For all the world to see

God is crying, tears of joy
Someone's gotten through
Lord I knew, you'd help this boy
Now I know just what to do

Take each day, for what it is
And all that it can be
Learn to give, what I can give
And understand, that I am free

Have compassion, for thy neighbor
Love the most that I can love
Never doubt, or even wonder
That there is someone up above

Birth of a Poem

Waiting for a miracle
That just may never happen
As I sit here with a blank page
Imagination, and a black pen

What should I write about?
Is it planned? Or does it flow?
Is there a certain process?
To go about, I don't know

I just want to write a poem
Maybe long, maybe short
Can you please tell me
Where now should I start?

Now I take the cap off my pen
And wait for what? I don't know
Then something comes over me
As my vision starts to grow

Words are scribbled
Some meanings unsure
But, they must stay put
Hand just moving, reality aware of no more

Eyes are blurred, and mind in deep
Thoughts are drawing pictures
A mirage of what I write about
Steal away the scriptures

Reaching the middle, the vision suddenly stops
I feel lost, how will it end?
So I put on my cap
I now must rest my pen

As the time goes by, I read what I've got
And instincts tell me when to resume
Until that time, it's an unfinished poem
With half a life, someday to be finished, I assume

Superstitions

Knock on wood, people say
Such a silly superstition
But if they must, let them knock
It's funny to me, but that's their position

Make sure you don't walk under a ladder
To me that sounds so crazy
But if they feel safe, with their little clause
Let it be, but that sounds so crazy

Never cross the path of a black cat
But it's just a little kitty
Now this one's weird, I really think
You shouldn't be afraid of a cat, what a pity

Everything it comes in threes
Now this one goes back to the birds and the bees
If you have twins, is that to say
That there's another one on the way

A pinch of salt, over your shoulder
And that will keep you safe
This superstition thing, that people play
Is such a silly game

Paint It Blue

You can paint it blue
But, I will paint it red
The color of roses, I'll give to you
To cheer you up instead

But, once the petals flew away
You wanted to paint it blue again

Well, you can paint it blue
But, I will paint it yellow
Getting down on one knee
Asking to be your fellow

I sensed relief, and seen you smile
And knew my efforts were all worthwhile

We had a lot of fun
We joked and laughed and kissed
Then time went by, you found another
The times we had, I really missed

Well now, you don't paint it blue anymore
But, now I paint it black
I look to see that you're not there
And you're not coming back

Leave a Light On

Leave a light on while I'm gone
Just in case I don't come back
It always seems you drift away
While slipping through the cracks

You always kept me standing
But I always seemed to fall
I always thought, that you would stay
Now I know that I was wrong

When blindness takes you over
It's kind of hard to see
And if you think that something's wrong
Then blame it all on me

If that's what makes you feel good
Then go for what you know
The things in life that feel so right
Make sure you take it slow

So I will fly, you do the same
And as we go we'll learn
Next time you need to pass the toll
The bridges won't be burned

Alright to Leave

Life means many little things
And the ones who achieve their goals
Are the ones who dare to dream

"Stupendous," I want to hear them say
"That man was more than something special"
Imbedded in my heart, his words will always stay

I want to be the one, who stands above the crowd
And put in all my everything
And every extra ounce of pride

I want to go where no one's gone
And even go beyond
I want to yell my name out loud
And scream it, to carry on

I want to bring you beyond the stars
To a galaxy of yet unknown
And then touchdown into despair
And then I'll bring you home

Bring you to a warm summer's day
Then polar glaciers melting
Make you feel, emotions, alive
Put your hand on my heart, and you can feel it beating

Read my words, if you feel me there
That's all I wanted to achieve
And if you felt what I conveyed
Then I'll know when it's my time, that it's alright to leave

Shoo! Fly

The fly is buzzing on the wall
I roll my paper up
I swing and miss and curse and swear
The fly, it flies into my cup

And just as I go to take a sip
The fly, it lands upon my nose
I punch myself right in the face
And quickly now I start to doze

And then I drift into a dream
Now I'm a spider, and I want to eat that bastard
He flies in circles
As I run faster

That annoying little creature
Really pisses me off
I spin my web, he's flying toward it
And then I start to cough

Suddenly now I am awake
And I have no cares about the fly
He's just something I should ignore
Why he consumed me, I don't know why?

The moral here is plain to see
Little things should be overlooked
Before your temper gets out of hand
Just calm down, before your goose is cooked

Lonely Echo

Sometimes the world is lonely
And some of god 's creatures feel neglected
But most of them just hang on to hope
It's a busy life, and things get hectic

But you must keep in mind
That back in days of old
People fought and built this country
To be free, and to be bold

Many gestures pardoned
Many sorry's, forgive me sir
Many nights lie wondering
What would represent our bird

Neither any, neither or
Neither why (I don't want to be poor)
What forsakes, what I can give
What's to say, that I can't live

Remember how the people fell
The blackest day, a living hell
But somehow humanity stayed alive
We can't be crutched, we must survive

So in a world that's oh so lonely
I'll tell you what is lonely, jack!
When you yell into the canyon grand
And your echo stays, and never comes back

Vicarious Destiny

I lie here in the dead of night
My body numb, and cannot breathe
I'll have to reach inside of me
'Cause I refuse to leave

Plagued with every ailment
One could not imagine
Walking through a hazy fog
Church bells all are bangin'

Calling me to come on home
But my soul will never rest
I haven't fulfilled my destiny in life
I must complete the quest

I run around in nights so calm
I yell but no one hears me
I think that I got left behind
Must find a way, to set me free

I put my words, in someone's head
And then he writes them down
He can't explain just where they came from
But his hand moves, so he calls them his own

Meanwhile I am working towards
Realizing freedom, from this pain
It now is time that I take flight
But someday, I'll be back again

Santa Claus Is Real

Santa Claus is real
I bet you didn't know that
The beard, the belt, the jolly old soul
The rosy cheeks, right up to his hat

Did you ever ask for something
And make a wish on Christmas Eve
And wake to daylight past the dawn
And it was there, could you believe

It's thought to be not
And not to be thought
He steals the cookies
But never gets caught

How does his suit ever stay clean
If he climbs on down the chimney
It must be magic, it's in the air
Just ask little Jimmy

One night he woke and heard a noise
Then went to see what's going on
And just as he approached the corner
There was a flash, and then it was gone

Even though he didn't see
The man, the myth, the legend
He proudly says that he believes
And doesn't have to pretend

The Day That Hell Froze Over

Rolling through a wasteland
That once was occupied
Visions grow within my nightmares
See a pair of evil eyes

I'm sure this land was fruitful once
I'd like to know what happened
A man so old I've never seen
Said, "Sit right down and listen"

I'll tell you what had happened here
I remember, as it was yesterday
That day I felt a cold wind blow
And little children ceased to play

And all the rockets sounded off
And all the noise, too loud to hear
Blinding lights they hurt my vision
People scrambling, all in fear

Time has left its mark on me
By letting me remember
That's the day that hell froze over
In that blustery cold December

I want to leave this awful place
Please let me off this giant rock
So roll me up into a ball
And put me in a big black box

Over the Edge

Rage and mercy, within I struggle
Scars they bleed upon my face
Take thy anger, world enflamed
Waste of life, such a disgrace

Point of impact, speeds unheard of
Smacking down to concrete fields
Daggers, sickles, razor sharp
Valley of the dancing seals

Stampeding, charging, marching on
Breaking out of heaven's shell
Gasp for air, when all is empty
Remnants of a place called hell

Revenge, misled, uncertainty
The killer's on the loose
But is he really out of sight
Or is the killer inside me and you

If I find the culprit
That pisses on my grave
Not one piece, will anyone find
Insanity, rage, has left me enslaved

Far beyond, far away
I'm never coming back
Fire burns, but not my skin
The core of vengeance, molten, crack!

Can Dreams Come True?

My dreams all filled up in a bottle
And sailed away to sea
The hours turned into days and nights
Waiting for them to come back for me

The moon comes up, the sun goes down
Another niche, the world turns 'round
The wakes they bellow with anticipation
Will the cork fly off and leave my dreams, at another station?

Look yonder past the horizon
Look yonder past the sea
And then a voice inside me says, "Believe in yourself
And your dreams will become reality"

So I left the spot for which I stood
A thousand days and nights
And continued on my merry way
Down the joyous road of life

To my surprise, I went back to
The very spot I stood
My dreams came back, and filled my heart
And then I understood

Once I Saw You Standing

A part of me has left my soul
And now it feels there's nowhere to go
Like a dream, time felt so brief
You stole my heart, just like a thief

Just who will fill this hole, you left inside my heart
I'll let you back, the missing piece
Then one lonely starry night
Once again the puzzle will be complete

A shadow in the distance
Could that just be you
I've suffered through the wars of hell
Skin is braised, and scorched me too

Throw me down a rope
And please help pull me up
'Cause I'm too weak to climb alone
Stand by me and be my crutch

I will learn to walk again
If you could just forgive
I give myself, a whole to you
Without you I can't live

Time is running short
I need to hear your voice
I'm falling now, and losing grip
Emptiness, without a choice

Be my eyes, be my guide
Let me off this nowhere ride
If you stand tall enough for both
I'll feel you pulling on the rope

Energy and just a slight pulse
I'm coming back to life
But it's too late, a marker laid
Words are blurred and cannot read
It says my name, can I believe
Once I saw you standing
Once I saw you leave

Drowning Inside

I reached for your hand
But the current pulled you under
The winds they swirled, black is the world
Hand of doom, feel my thunder

I tried to pull you up
But fate would not permit
I reached, and stretched, and cried like hell
I promised you, I'd never quit

I could almost swear, I touched your hand
And seen a vision of me and you
We were halfway to heaven
And there's the gate, we're going through

But wait, just when we start to enter
Someone pulls me back
And says, "It's not your time yet"
Keep your life on track

But you went through
And I didn't understand
How you gave up and died inside
And I stood tall, just like a man

I sat and sobbed beside myself
And wore a crooked frown
Not knowing you gave up long ago
Before the water touched you, you had already drowned

You were drowning inside
But, I couldn't see
The selfishness inside of you
Encapturing a part of me

So if I grabbed your hand
And held on real tight
It wouldn't have mattered anyway
It tore me up, you quit the fight

So don't call my name
If you won't try to swim
Some lights they burn, so bright sometimes
Sometimes they turn so dim

Wasted Time

Wasted time in life I see
Compiles and builds another me
Many mountains, high and low
Raging river, where shall I go
Choices, choices, all around us
Can't you hear the voices call us
Seek me out, find my path
Hide me from the evil's wrath
If I swam for days and nights
And days and nights again
My body cold and numb before you
Would I recall where I began
I will go now out to sea
And prove my journey done
Next time I will try much harder
Next time I will be the one

A Poet's Pain

No one knows a poet's pain
Sometimes the tears, they fall like rain
Bottled up, so no one sees
The anguish caused from misery
Swept away, I shall not return
To face the coils, I have been burned
Like a dream, you're here, then gone
When memories hurt, I can't go on
To bleed the blood, I'd bleed for you
The salt from tears, it stings my wounds
I'd never leave you all alone
But alone left am I
So chosen in my mind I choose
Nothing left, I must die
I gave you all, you gave me none
I searched the world, to find someone
A king's ransom in gold
A piece of my soul
A hole in my heart
Now that we are apart

Invisible

Hey now, hey now
Can't you see me standing here?
You pushed me to the limit
And treat me like you just don't care

I have motivation
And I have steel will
But one thing that does bother me
Your comments, how they kill

Oh, someday you'll glance at the sky
And see me hangin' from a star
At one with all the galaxy
You'll see me from afar

And you will never reach me
And neither will your words
Blow your breath into the wind
And save it for the birds

All I asked, that you believe
But you were full of doubt
And just when heaven shows its light
You're the one left out

So build your wall, as high as hell
And don't let no one in
And in the end, you'll soon find out
It won't be you who wins

So open up your mind
And open up your soul
Curiosity's need an answer
This is one thing, you should know

The road I choose to travel
Will all have curves and bends
And yours will tend to fork and split
And eventually end up…
    Dead End.

Fly Me Away

If I could only, for just one day
Meet you on the other side
I wouldn't stand a chance in this world
'Cause I think I'd never want to leave
and that, my dear, I can't deny

'cause living in this world
it's alright and it's okay
but to dine with thee above the clouds
would take my sorrows away

sometimes I feel like leaving
when I stare at your photograph
and it echoes in my mind
I could still hear your voice
And the way that you laughed

Please take me with you
Don't leave me here alone
Fly me away beyond the stars
Beyond the thunder dome

I want to be there by your side
But will you still be there
When the angels fly me to the sky
And I walk up heaven's stairs

Hush, my love, don't say a word
I'll set your mind at ease
All systems clear for takeoff
I think I'm gonna leave

Fly me away beyond the stars
Beyond the thunder dome
Meet me halfway in heaven
I think I'm coming home

Solitaire

When you notice no one's there
That my friend is solitaire

Speaking from your inner thoughts
Buying books that weren't bought
Spending time, then stop and stare
Many forms of solitaire

If Adam never found his Eve
Then what would there be left to leave
No Romeo for Juliet
What would be left I can't forget

Would little children ever play
If solitaire was once a day

Would company be such a word
Or couple, mean to be unheard

Inside I roam around awhile
It's black as black can be
Searching for the story told
Of what will never be

Solitaire, oh! Solitaire
Tell me why your name I hear
Why must you have chosen me
What will now be thinketh of me

Guardian Heart

Please, let me touch your heart
I know I really can
I felt it beating faster, harder
Then you pushed away my hands

I had the key, but couldn't find
The lock that it would fit
I saw your eyes, and time stood still
Something told me, this is it

Journey to the brightest lands
Distant deep blue seas
Feel the warmth of sun and sky
Breeze beneath the trees

Lost within a great collage
Of beauty, colors, bliss
Surrounded by the innocence
Of just a simple kiss

I stormed the castle, fast and swift
And tried to climb the wall
I scaled it, brick by brick
But you built it way too tall

I asked the guard to let me in
But he did not reply
He never learned to speak at all
Instead he only cried

I've seen the tears and figured out
That they would melt the wall
Imagining, and deep in thought
The wall began to fall

And then a glow, beyond the gates
And then I saw, a beautiful face

Welcoming with open arms
A smile, what a sight
Flowing hair, I hear a heartbeat
Showing signs of life

Please, let me touch your heart
I know I really can
Because a heart that has no love
Could never beat again

I'll Be There

When you feel that no one cares
Turn around and I'll be there
When you feel that you can't see
I'll be there behind the trees
Feeling lost or left alone
I'll be there to guide you home
When the answer seems out of sight
I'll be there in the dead of the night
When there's no love left for you
I'll share mine, yes that I'll do
And when you want, but cannot get
I'll be there, just don't forget

Poem for a Friend

Such is this, such is life
Such is so must wasted
Take the time to look around
You've left a lot untasted

A world you've traveled
And seen some sights
But your path was narrow
The bells would jingle on Christmas night

But you stayed away
Didn't believe to celebrate
To have your own beliefs is fine
It never meant that you did hate

A friend to the end
You were always there
When I said help, you always did
You always opened up to share

I heard the news
And hung my head
'Cause someone told me
That you was dead

I'll see you on the other side
Even if you thought that not
"Oh! Boy, what a life"
Your words will never be forgot

(My Father) The Hero

Went and fought in Vietnam
Earned a Purple Heart
Came home and had a couple of kids
Tried to leave the trauma behind and make a brand-new start

Then the day came, she went and left him
She, meaning my mother, left him for another man
I didn't know what was going on, I was young
I tried to leave with him, and she said I can

Then she changed her mind, said that she was drunk
Told me I'd be nothing in life
But he, meaning my father, said I would be something
So time it passed, and I did grow
And I always remember, my father, the hero!

My Hair

Circumstances beyond our control
We won't be going home
My hair it sways from left to right
I think I need a comb

I don't know how we got to this place
But I feel so much despair
And the only thing that's on my mind
I can't stop thinking 'bout my hair

It just sits atop my head
Never knowing which way to part
It stands straight up into the sky
Every time I blow a fart

War pigs crawling, people dying
The world is getting crazy
I haven't combed my hair for weeks
I must be getting lazy

I've seen the greatness in this world
I've ran with all the best
My fingers always get so oily
When I run them through this nest

With all the things to worry about
In a world that doesn't care
I can't believe the only thing that's on my mind
Is my stupid fuckin' hair

ABOUT THE AUTHOR

Billy J. Barnum is a direct descendant of the famous Phineas Taylor Barnum, aka P. T. Barnum The Greatest Showman on Earth. He grew up in humble beginnings and found his love for writing songs and poetry in his early teens. He would often write poems and recite them for his friends and family and was amazed at their reaction after listening to him speak. They would say such things like "Wow! Did you write that? That sounds like Shakespeare!" Hence the title of the book.

Legend says that because of their encouraging words and reactions that the birth of this book was born. Billy also is a collector of sports cards and has quite a collection. Billy currently resides in Connecticut where his children live as well. He loves to go to Cape Cod on vacations as it's close to his location, and he admires the scenery and awesome historic lighthouses that Cape Cod offers.

Billy has had the poems you are about to read locked away for years and years and has finally decided to take a leap of faith and publish them for your reading enjoyment. He hopes that some of the poems inspire you and other poems make you profoundly think of the world around you. Through his imagination and words, he also hopes that your imagination will inspire you to do great things.

CPSIA information can be obtained
at www.ICGtesting.com
Printed in the USA
BVHW041924070120
568848BV00011B/368/P